TARANGINI

Swami Chinmayananda
and
Swamini Saradapriyananda

CENTRAL CHINMAYA MISSION TRUST

Total no. of copies printed up to June 2006 - 25000 copies
Second Edition June 2011 - 3000 copies
Third Edition January 2013 to December 2020 - 11,250 copies
Reprint August 2024 - 1,500 copies

Published by:
Chinmaya Prakashan
The Publications Division of
Central Chinmaya Mission Trust
Sandeepany Sadhanalaya
Saki Vihar Road, Mumbai 400072, India
Tel.: +91-22-2803 4900
Email: ccmtpublications@chinmayamission.com
Website: www.chinmayamission.com

Distribution Centre in the USA:
Chinmaya Publications West
560 Bridgetown Pike
Feasterville, PA 19053-7240, USA
Tel.: (215) 396-0390, Fax: (215) 396-9710
Email: publications@chinmayamission.org
Website: www.chinmayapublications.com

Design and Illustrations: Blue Fish

Printed by: Thomson Press (India) Ltd., Faridabad

ISBN: 978-81-7597-521-7

CONTENTS

1. The Test 1

2. Word with Authority 4
3. The Two Gems 8
4. Initiation 13
5. The Three Questions 15
6. Confidence 20
7. Ramanuja and the Sacred Mantra 25
8. Visoba Khechera 29
9. Gautam Buddha 34

10. The Rishi's Dilemma 38
11. Corrupt Officials 40
12. The Needle 42
13. Dharmavyadha 45
14. Wisdom and Action 51
15. The Mirror (One-Act Play) 54
16. Savitri (One-Act Play) 66

- Code of Conduct for the Chinmaya Mission Members 79
- Chinmaya Mission Pledge 80

Listen!
Ye Children of Immortal Bliss!

The Test

Once there was a debate among the sages as to who was the greatest amongst the trinity of gods, that is— Brahma, Vishnu and Maheswara. They could not decide. So they asked Bhrigu Maharshi to undertake this test.

Bhrigu Maharshi consented and went first to Brahma-loka. Brahma, the Creator, was in his durbar. He did not greet or welcome Bhrigu. Bhrigu took a seat without offering salutations to the Creator.

Brahma felt insulted. All the three worlds respected him as the Creator. Here was a mere sage from the world of human beings who was sitting there without having saluted him! He became angry and very red in the face, but controlled himself and did not say anything to the sage. Bhrigu noticed it all and went away.

Bhrigu then went to Kailasa. At that time Siva was dancing with Parvati. When he saw Bhrigu standing there without prostrating before him, Siva got furious and lifted his trident to kill the sage. Parvati rushed forward and caught hold of the trident. She calmed Siva and advised him that it would not be proper to kill a sage. Bhrigu took note of this as well and walked out.

His next destination was Vaikuntha. Vishnu was reclining on his snake-bed. He kicked Vishnu on His chest and shouted in great rage, "How dare you sleep when I come?"

Vishnu sat up with a start. When he saw the sage standing before him, he got up and prostrated before the Rishi with great reverence. Massaging the foot with which he had been kicked, he said softly, "Revered Sir, please excuse me for being asleep when you came. Your foot must have been hurt when it came in contact with my chest. Let me massage it and relieve your pain."

Bhrigu Maharshi smiled and left. Bhrigu then went back to the rishis and gave a detailed description

of what had happened in the three worlds. He said, "Brahma is rajasika. He is full of ego and was angry when I did not salute him. Siva is tamasika. He not only got angry but was ready to kill me, for the simple reason that I did not salute him. Vishnu is sattvika. He apologised, even though the fault was mine. He is the best. Let us offer the fruit of our sacrifice to him."

Thus there are no temples dedicated to Brahma in this world. Siva is worshipped only in the form of a linga. But in every city or town in this country there are temples dedicated to Vishnu in his various avataras.

Word with Authority

Once there was a king who did not know any philosophy. As he became older, his interest in philosophy grew and he wanted to study the scriptures. His minister was well-read and a good philosopher too. So the king asked his minister to teach him.

The minister replied, “Maharaj, I am not the right person to teach you philosophy. It will be better if you study the texts from my Guru.”

The king laughed and said, “Mantriji, what are you talking about? The scriptural text is the same, whether you explain it or your Guru does. Why should I trouble your Guru?"

The minister said, "Maharaj, indeed, it makes a difference. If you take the trouble to come to my house tomorrow, I will prove it to you."

Accordingly, the king went to the minister's house the next day. The minister received him with all due respect and offered him a seat of honour.

The minister sat on a lower seat and started conversation. Their discussion was general at first. Soon the minister started disagreeing with what the king said and the two got into an argument.

Thereupon, the minister got angry. He turned to his servant and ordered, "Arrest the king and bind his hands and feet!"

The servant was aghast! The minister ordering the arrest of the king! He dared not budge from his place.

The minister said again, "Arrest him. Haven't you heard me?"

The servant still did not move. The minister repeated the order two or three times. But the servant stood still and did not obey. The king, who was witnessing all this in utter amazement, became angry at the impertinence of the minister. How dare he order the king's arrest!

The king looked at the servant and said sternly, "Arrest this impertinent minister and bind his hands and feet."

That very moment the servant sprang into action.

He immediately arrested the minister and, taking a rope, firmly tied his hands and feet.

The minister smiled and said to the king, "Maharaj see, the difference between us! When I ordered him the servant did not obey me. But when you ordered, he obeyed you immediately. The authority is in the person and not in the words. The same is the case with philosophy. Even though I understand the scriptures, I am not an authority on them. When my Guru speaks, he speaks with authority and conviction. That is why I did not wish to teach you philosophy."

The king understood. He too smiled happily and ordered the release of the minister. Later, he approached the minister's Guru and was initiated by him into the practice of philosophical truths.

The Two Gems

King Vikramarka was a great king, renowned for his valour, kindness and charitable disposition. He never kept anything for himself but gave away to others even the rarest and most priceless objects.

Once, Bali Chakravarty, who dwelt in Patala, heard of him. As he himself was of a charitable nature, he wished to see what Vikramarka was like, and arranged for the king's visit to Patala. Vikramarka considered it a rare privilege to visit Patala and spend some time with Bali, who was also very famous.

Their meeting gave them mutual satisfaction. After remaining there for a few months,

Vikramarka took leave of Bali. At the time of parting, Bali presented him with two rare gems. He asked Vikramarka to keep them for himself, saying that they were precious stones with magical powers.

When Vikramarka came back to earth he found himself in a thick forest very far from his kingdom, and set out to find his way through the forest. Soon it became dark and so he decided to take rest under a tree for the night.

In the middle of the night he was awakened by someone talking nearby, under the next tree. Evidently there were two persons, who appeared to be related to one another as father and son. They were discussing their family problems—poverty, girls of marriageable age, and so on. From their talk

Vikramarka understood that they had been to his court to seek his help, but not finding him there, they were returning disappointed. He decided to help them in the morning.

As soon as he got up in the morning, he remembered what he had heard the night before. He turned to see whether the father and the son were still there. He found them there. They had finished their morning ablutions and were about to leave the place.

Vikramarka addressed them

without disclosing who he was, and said, "Sirs, please excuse me. Last night I couldn't help overhearing your conversation. I understand that because of poverty, you are unable to perform the marriages required in your family. Please don't worry that you didn't meet King Vikramarka. Here are two magical gems. One gem bestows on the owner as much money as he wants. The other gem gives youth. Please take whichever gem you want."

The son was very happy. He jumped up in joy at the offer and said, "Thank you, Sir. You appear to be as charitable as Vikramarka himself. Please give us the gem that gives the money. We need it to marry off my sisters."

But the father interfered and told his son, "Do not be in a hurry. In matters of this kind, one must think clearly. Let us consider the matter carefully before we select the gem. Come, let us talk."

The son was surprised. What was there to discuss? They had gone to the king's court for money. Now here it was being offered by some unknown philanthropist. Why not grab the chance and take what they want?

The father dragged his son to a place where they could discuss in privacy and said, "Son, you don't know what a miserable experience old age is. I am so old now that I can't enjoy anything in life. Please let us take the gem which gives youth as I would still like to enjoy life."

The son was dumbfounded. Had his father lost

his senses? Six of his sisters were unmarried as they had no money to get them married and here was his father who wished to become young again! He vehemently opposed his father and said that they should take the gem that gave money and solve their present problems. The father begged, but the son was adamant. Neither of them agreed to the other's point of view. As they discussed and argued, the kindhearted Vikramarka understood their conflict.

He called out to them, "Sirs," he said with a kind smile, "I understand what you are discussing. Don't worry about choosing one gem. Here are the gems. Take them both and be happy."

The father and son were extremely happy. They took both the gems, praised the unknown donor and went away singing his praises. Vikramarka had once again proved that the generosity of his heart knew no bounds.

Initiation

As a young boy, Saint Kabir Das was brought up by his father in the traditional Muslim way. However, he also found great beauty in Hinduism and wanted to be initiated by Swami Ramananda, a great sage of Banaras. In those days society was rigid and it was unthinkable for a Muslim boy to approach a Hindu sage for initiation. Yet, the young devout heart yearned for initiation by the sage. He thought deeply about the matter and at last found a way to fulfill his heart's desire without the great man even knowing about it.

Unknown to Swami Ramananda, Kabir observed his habits closely and found that the Guru went every day to bathe in the Ganges at a very early hour when it was still very dark.

One day the young boy woke up before it was time for the Guru's bath. He went to the bathing ghat and secretly lay down upon the steps of the ghat leading to the river. It was still very dark, so no one could see him. At the usual time Swami Ramananda came down the steps. As he slowly climbed down the steps, his feet touched Kabir's body. Swamiji knew that someone was lying there. He immediately withdrew his foot and uttered 'Rama, Rama'.

Joyously Kabir jumped up, exclaiming, "Blessed am I indeed, O Guru, that you have initiated me into the Rama-nama. I am your disciple."

Swami Ramananda was taken aback. But he understood Kabir's deep desire to walk on the spiritual path. He accepted him as his disciple. At last the student, thirsty for knowledge, had found a teacher, and the teacher a diligent student.

The Three Questions

Once a king had three doubts which concerned his day-to-day life. He asked many people but no one could provide him with satisfactory answers. His questions were—What is the most important thing to be done? Who should be considered the most important person? What is the most important gain?

Vexed by his unanswered questions, the king became very restless. Then he heard that on a certain mountain near his kingdom, lived a great sage. He was very wise and would be able to give him satisfactory answers. The king decided to meet the sage.

So one afternoon, he mounted his horse and went galloping to the mountain. When he reached the foot of the mountain, he tied the horse to a tree and began climbing up. The sage's ashram was at the top, and the king gasped for breath as he struggled up. On reaching the top he found the sage working very hard. He was digging with a spade and throwing out the loose earth by carrying it in baskets. The sage was very old and yet he was working so hard!

The king went near the sage and prostrated before him. He introduced himself, asked his three questions and begged him for answers. The sage didn't reply but went on with his work. The king respectfully waited on one side. As he watched he felt the Sage's tiredness. Sweat poured from his limbs. His face was all wrinkled. The

king thought, he is so old. I am young. Maybe I should help. He took the spade from the sage's hand and started digging himself. The sage sat down to rest.

The king continued to work for two or three hours. By then it was evening and darkness had descended. Just then, they heard the footsteps of someone walking with great difficulty. They turned their heads to see a man who was panting and gasping. His chest was blood-stained. The king rushed forward to hold the man and prevented him from falling.

The sage told the king, "Please bring him into the ashram." The king carried him inside. He gently laid the man on the cot and removed his shirt and examined his wound. The wound was very serious. As the man had lost much blood he was exhausted. The king cleaned the wound and put a bandage over it. He helped the man to drink some milk. That night the king slept on the floor next to the wounded man, getting up whenever he required assistance.

By the morning the man was better and was able to sit up in the bed. The king enquired about his health and attended to all his needs. After a good meal, the patient gained some strength. He rose from his bed and fell at the feet of the king and begged his pardon.

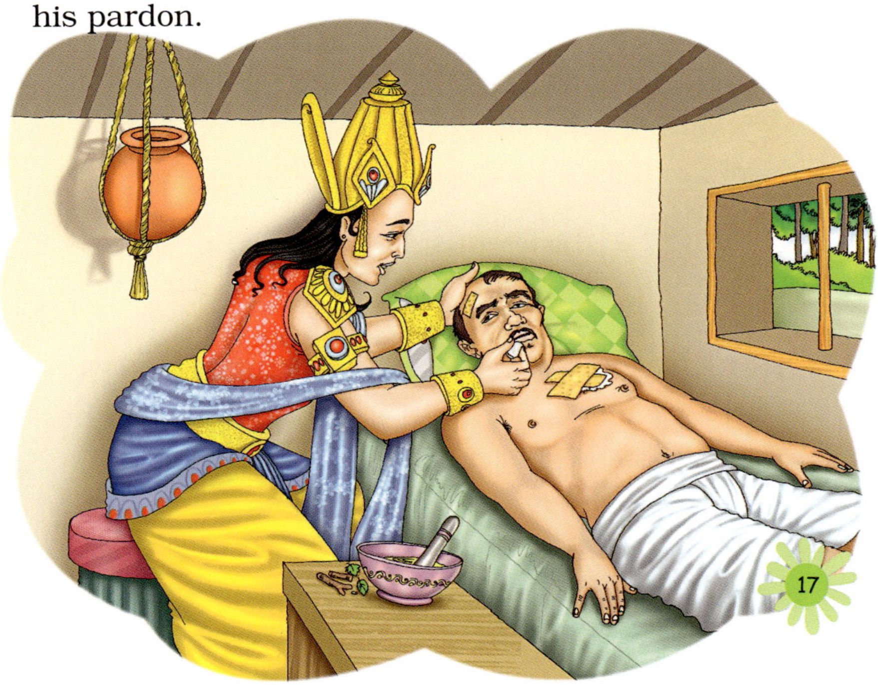

The surprised king lifted him up and asked, “Why do you beg pardon of me?”

The man replied, “O good King, know that I am one of the spies employed by your enemy to kill you stealthily. I saw you climbing the mountain all by yourself. Hoping to catch you alone and murder you, I followed you. My own enemy, who saw me coming up, thrust his sword into my chest and wounded me. Helplessly I came up and you so lovingly looked after me and saved me from death. Henceforth I swear to remain faithful to you and help you in all your needs. Please accept me as your friend.” The king embraced him with affection and accepted his friendship.

Now it was the king’s turn to take leave of the sage. While prostrating to the sage, he repeated his three questions and asked, “O Sage, I am much bothered by these three doubts and had come to you for the answers. Please set my mind at rest.”

The sage smiled and said, “King, you answered all your three questions by yourself yesterday. Why do you ask me?”

Looking at the surprised face of the king, the sage continued, “Yesterday when you came here, you found me sweating and working very hard. You took pity on me and helped me, forgetting everything else. The most important thing is to do the work which comes to you at that time. You benefitted from what you did yesterday. You were delayed in returning home, and so escaped the enemy's secret attack. Otherwise you would have been a dead man now. This is the answer to your first question.

"When the wounded man came to us, you forgot me and your comforts, and attended to his needs. This is the answer to the second question. The man in front of you is the most important man. You attended to him, forgetting the rest. This helped you yesterday because he dropped his enmity towards you and became your friend.

"A friend gained and an enemy conquered by love is the most important gain of all. By your loving services your enemy became your friend. There is no greater gain in the world than this. Had you fought with your enemy and killed him, it would not have been a positive gain for you. Now you have a lifelong friend."

Satisfied with the replies given by the sage, the king took leave of the sage and went back to his kingdom with his mind at rest. He ruled wisely and confidently, both qualities coming from the knowledge that he was doing the right thing.

Confidence

Once a tribal girl from the Himalayas called Bhagirathi was wedded to a man from another tribe of the same region, dwelling in another valley. When she came to live with her husband, she discovered to her dismay, that there was no water supply in their village, and that everybody had to go four miles in order to get water for their daily needs. In her parental village they had plenty of water and this new life, where water had to be sparingly used, was very difficult for her.

After some time, when she became familiar with her in-laws and others in the tribe, she suggested to them, "Why don't we dig a well in our colony?"

They all laughed at her as if it was a foolish notion. For generations they had lived in the same place. No one had ever thought of digging a well. Now a new bride suggested it. Everyone made fun of her and did not even consider the idea worth any attention.

But Bhagirathi did not give up. She did not say anything more to her elders but whenever young women of her own age went together to get water, she would slowly sow the seeds of the new idea into their minds. "How nice it would be to have a well of our own in our colony! Then we wouldn't have to come such a long distance. We would be able to get water at any time of the day."

As time passed, the other girls too started feeling like Bhagirathi. One day she suggested, "Instead of sitting and talking in the afternoons, suppose we start digging a well in our colony?"

The others thought that it was a wonderful idea. Some day the well would be deep enough to find water. The idea caught their imagination. Every one of them was thrilled. They started thinking of ways and means of achieving this. First of all they would keep it secret from the elders and the men, because they were sure to laugh at their attempts. When the well would get ready and water filled it, there would be sufficient time for the others to see what the girls had achieved.

Thus they planned everything secretly. There was a thrill in their secrecy. They selected a suitable place in the colony, and got to work. What was the proper time for them to go digging? In the afternoons the men would be away in the fields. The older women would be having their nap. That would be the best time because they would have three to four hours of spare time then.

One fine afternoon, the young women, armed with shovels and spades, marched to the place selected

by them. They said a short prayer to the Lord and started digging. The soil was rocky and very hard, but they went on with determination. The first day they could hardly dig one yard deep. The second day it was easier as they had practice. Within a week the entire younger generation of the village was involved. But none of the elders knew about it. One day, one of the older women woke up early and was surprised to find her daughter-in-law absent. She went to the next house to see whether she was there but found that their daughter-in-law too was missing. The elders asked each other and soon discovered the whereabouts of the youngsters. By then, the well was already twenty feet deep and the girls sang, laughed and worked joyously like bees in a honeycomb. The elders were pleasantly surprised.

Here was some positive work on hand. So they too began to lend a hand. Now the pace of the work was further accelerated. In a few days, the well was fifty feet deep.

When the men came to know about the work, it had to be dug only another twenty or thirty feet more. Now the well was a certainty and no more a fantasy. The men too were serious. Why not help on Sundays? The men saw with admiration what their feeble women had achieved and they worked for three Sundays.

One day suddenly there was a joyous cry, 'Water, water!' The sweet nectarine water came from underneath and gradually filled the bottom of the well.

The whole colony gathered there to celebrate the event. What a relief it was for everyone! Now they did not have to go four miles to get a pot of water. It was within their reach, day and night. Also, it was all the more precious because they had got it with their own efforts.

Faith in oneself and in the result of the work of one and all is bound to be blessed by the Lord!

Ramanuja and the Sacred Mantra

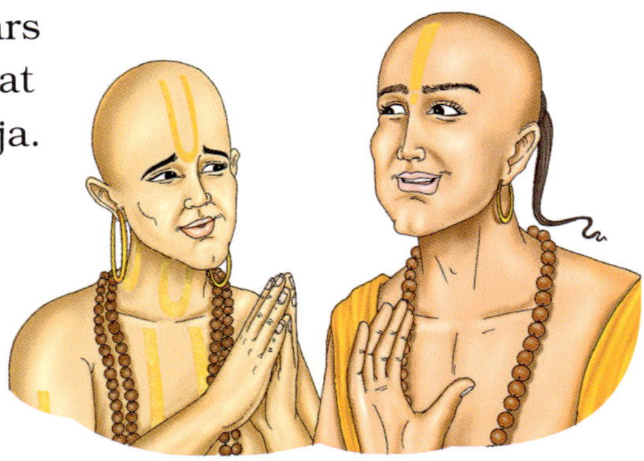

Several hundred years ago, there lived a great saint called Ramanuja. One day, he went to meet another saint, Sri Goshtipurna. He asked him for a deeksha mantra which would mark his formal initiation into spirituality. Goshtipurna refused Ramanuja and sent him away. But Ramanuja did not give up. He went to the master again and again and begged him for deeksha, but Goshtipurna was adamant. Ramanujacharya wept in despair. He thought that he must be really unworthy to have been refused the mantra eighteen times!

One day the priest of Sriranganatha temple met Goshtipurna and informed him that the Lord wanted him to initiate Ramanuja, into the mantra.

Goshtipurna did not hesitate any more. He gave the mantra to Ramanuja and explained its meaning with all its implications. He instructed Ramanuja to keep the mantra a secret as it was a powerful mantra. It had the power to give an immediate vision of Vaikuntha to the initiated. Ramanuja prostrated before the Guru and left. The very initiation sent a thrill through his whole being and he was blessed with a vision of the abode of the Lord, as promised by the Guru.

Thrilled to the core, he felt such peace and joy that he wanted to share it with everyone. He climbed the gopuram of the Sriranganatha temple and shouted, "My dear friends, come one and all. I shall tell you the great name that gives the vision of the Lord. Come, do not hesitate."

Fascinated by his beaming face and sincere words, several people gathered around him. Then he gave them the mantra which had been given

to him in great secrecy by his Guru. A wave of joy passed through the listeners and more and more people gathered to receive the mantra from him. Thus the name of the Lord spread far and wide.

Someone reported this to Goshtipurna. He was infuriated on hearing that Ramanuja had transgressed his specific instruction to not to give the mantra to anyone. What did he mean by shouting it from rooftops to the entire public?

Exactly at that time, Ramanuja, with a beaming face came there with his disciples. Goshtipurna shouted at him in anger. "You are the vilest person

I have met, fit to be thrown into hell for violating the Guru's instructions."

Ramanujacharya prostrated with humility before the teacher and said, "True, my teacher, I deserve to go to hell for going against your instructions. I did it deliberately. What does it matter if one person like me goes to hell when so many persons can be helped to go to the Lord's abode? I am prepared to suffer for the sake of so many."

Looking at his face glowing with love for his fellow beings, Goshtipurna realised how great and selfless he was. He understood that here was a man chosen by the Lord as His instrument to lead many to salvation.

Goshtipurna forgot his anger. He embraced Ramanujacharya with love and blessed him.

Visoba Khechera

Namadeva was a great devotee of Lord Panduranga. The Lord himself would appear to him in person and talk to him. Namadeva could not tear himself away from the temple. He loved to be in the presence of the Lord.

Once, Jnanadeva and some other wise masters made fun of Namadeva for his attachment to the temple. Namadeva felt insulted by their discouraging talk of going to the temple to spend time with his beloved God. When Panduranga himself approved, why should others find fault with him, he thought. He came to his beloved and complained to him with tears in his eyes.

Panduranga wiped away his tears and embracing him, said sweetly, "Leave them alone. But Namadeva, I want you to do one thing. There is a great jnani called Visoba Khechera in the village nearby. Go and receive instructions in spirituality from him. This is needed for your progress."

Tears started flowing from Namadeva's eyes at just the mention of leaving his Lord. He wept unconsolably, exclaiming, "My God my beloved, you are my all in all how can I live away from you?"

Panduranga gave Namadeva courage and strength. He patted him on the back, and cheered him up saying, "It is only for a few days. You will be back soon."

Namadeva could not refuse to go. Looking back again and again, biting his lips to prevent them from trembling, and uttering words of farewell, he went out of the temple. He left Pandharpur and reached the village indicated by Panduranga, on the third day. There he made enquiries about Visoba Khechera.

The villagers guided him to the Siva temple on the outskirts of the village where the sage resided. Namadeva went eagerly to meet the jnani recommended by Panduranga Himself. When he reached the temple, he found the doors open but found no one there. He went in and searched but still could find no one. But when he reached the inner shrine, he was shocked to find an old man lying inside with both his feet on the linga! Could this be he, to seek whom he was sent all the way from Pandharpur by the Lord himself?

Anger and irritation struggled within his bosom. He rushed into the shrine and woke up the old man by shaking him roughly by the shoulder. The old man slowly opened his eyes and saw Namadeva.

He asked in a low voice, "Son, why do you disturb my sleep?"

"Sleep, my foot! Do you know how you are sleeping? Your feet are on the Lord. Remove them immediately."

The old man looked at him calmly and said, "Is that so, son? I am an old man and can't get up easily. Please remove my feet and place them where the Lord is not."

Namadeva was furious with the old man. In a fit of anger he caught hold of the old man's feet and flung them in the direction opposite to the linga.

The old man did not protest at this rough treatment. His feet were about to touch the ground, when lo!, a linga sprang up from under the earth, as it were, a footrest for the old man's feet. Thus the feet were on a linga again! This was not the original linga but a new one. From where did the second one come? Namadeva rubbed his eyes to see whether he was dreaming. No, the second linga was very much there and could not be wished away.

He caught hold of the old man's feet again and put them in a third direction. Again, before the feet touched the ground another linga sprang up exactly as before. Namadeva tried again and again. Wherever he put the feet, a new linga sprang up. The whole place was full of lingas and there was no place where there was no linga.

Now where could he place the feet? Bewildered, he placed the feet on his own head, because at least no linga could spring up there, or so he thought. The moment the feet touched his head, he was illumined by their holy touch. In a flash he understood the all-pervading nature of the supreme Self. The sage whose feet purified him was a perfect jnani, who saw the Lord everywhere.

In utter shame and repentance, he fell at the feet of the old man who was none other than Visoba Khechera, and begged his pardon. Then he said in a humble tone, "Please give me wisdom. My beloved Lord Panduranga has sent me to you."

The sage smiled and said, "Now you know everything. Go back."

Namadeva took leave of him respectfully and came back to Pandharpur, feeling the presence of the Lord in everything, from a tiny blade of grass to the mighty mountains. After returning, he stayed at home and did not visit the temple. On the fourth day, when Namadeva still had not gone to the Lord, Panduranga Himself came and knocked at the door. "My dear Namadeva, please open the door and let me in. I have missed you and am longing to be with you once more."

Namadeva came to the door but he did not open it. He replied from within, "Ah, dear Lord, I know now what a trickster you are! You kept me deluded

into thinking that you were only in the temple. Now I know that you are everywhere. I see you in a mighty mountain and in a grain of sand. Indeed you are in the temple and outside it."

Panduranga laughed at his devotee's new found wisdom and blessed him for all times to come.

Gautam Buddha

When Prince Siddharth was born, astrologers told his father King Suddhodhana that the boy would become either a great king or a great sannyasin.

The father did not want him to become a sannyasin. So he brought him up carefully, without allowing him to see any sights which were likely to create dispassion in him. His palace was filled with young and energetic servants; the gardens were maintained in such a way that no dried plants were visible. When the king and the queen started aging, they dyed their hair black so that their son could not detect signs of old age. Thus the boy grew to the age of twenty-nine without knowing the facts of life.

He was married to a beautiful princess whose name was Yashodhara. They led a happy married life and soon a baby boy was born to them. Siddharth's life was now complete with every joy. One day, Siddharth wanted to visit the city. When the king was approached with the request, he fixed up a sight-seeing trip for him, making sure that no unhappy sights came his way when he was outside the palace.

But when he was out driving, Siddharth saw an old man bent double with age, walking slowly with the help of a stick. He was shocked at this sight. He asked Chenna, the charioteer, why the man walked in such a peculiar way.

Chenna replied, "O Prince, the man is very old."

"Really!" exclaimed the prince. "Do we all become old, Chenna?"

Chenna said, "Yes, Prince. One day we will all become old and feeble."

Siddharth became thoughtful. After a while he saw a sick man coming from the opposite direction, shivering and groaning. Again Siddharth asked, "Tell me, Chenna, why is this man behaving in such a strange way?"

Chenna replied, "The man is sick and is suffering."

Then Siddharth enquired, "Is sickness common to all?"

"Yes Prince, it is," said Chenna.

Siddharth became silent. Yet another scene met his eyes. This time it was a dead body being carried to the cremation ground. The prince was surprised to see a man, motionless and still, being carried on the shoulders of other men. Chenna told him that the man was dead but the prince found it difficult to understand. In one day he had learnt the bitter truths of life which had been hidden from him for twenty-nine years! As he pondered over what he had seen, he saw a recluse and also learnt for the first time that there were people who sought solutions to the problems of life through a life of renunciation. The calm and serene face of the recluse made a deep impression upon Siddharth and he returned to the palace, grave and thoughtful.

That night he could not sleep. What he had seen during the day kept him awake and thinking. After a while he rose from the bed. In the dead of night, he went to his wife's room to see her and his infant son for the last time. He gazed at them with love and then slowly crept out. Siddharth then woke Chenna and asked him to get his horse ready. He rode till he reached the outskirts of the city and was soon beyond the walls of the fort.

The faithful Chenna ran behind the horse. He tried to dissuade his master from taking the terrible step of renunciation, but there was no going back for Siddharth. He was determined to discover the root cause of all the sorrows of the world.

Siddharth wandered from place to place in search of enlightenment. He performed austerities for many years. In the end, under the shade of the Bodhi tree, he found answers to the questions that were tormenting him. Prince Siddharth then became Gautam Buddha, the Enlightened One.

The Rishi's Dilemma

Once upon a time, a rishi was doing penance in a forest. One day, a man came running to him in great terror. He was perspiring, both out of exertion and fear. Clutching the feet of the sage, he said, "Maharaj! I am in great peril. I am being pursued by a murderer. Please show me a way to escape from him."

The rishi took pity on him and pointed out an intricate path in the forest by which he

could escape. The man was grateful and ran along the path as fast as he could.

The rishi then closed his eyes and plunged himself in meditation. After some time a rough looking man, with a sword in hand, arrived. He paused before the holy man and asked, "Sir, have you seen a man running in this direction?"

The rishi was in a dilemma. If he said that he had seen the man, he would surely ask him which way he had gone. He would have had to point out the way to this murderer. That would be assisting the murder of a person. But to deny any knowledge of the man, would be a lie, and that was wrong. How could he avoid both?

The rishi thought for some time and replied, "My dear Sir, you are asking an impossible question. It is the eye that sees. You are asking the mouth to speak. The mouth does not see. How can the mouth say what the eye has seen?"

The rishi's reply appeared to be perfectly logical. The murderer was all brawn and no brain and could not see that the rishi was only trying to confuse him. Bewildered, he retraced his steps and went back. The Rishi thus saved a man's life without compromising his own principles of life.

Corrupt Officials

Once a corrupt official invited the scholar saint of Kerala, Chattambi Swamigal for bhiksha. Swamiji knew of the bad reputation of the official. He accepted his invitation and thought of a way to humble his vanity and pride. He told him that he would bring his disciples along with him for bhiksha. Accordingly, food was prepared for them as well.

On the appointed day of the bhiksha, Swamiji arrived alone. The host enquired about his disciples. Swamiji replied, "They are all waiting outside. As soon as the food is served, they will come in."

Food was served. Then Swamiji called out loudly, "Come in, my disciples."

To the horror of the official, a pack of street dogs walked in, one after another, in an orderly manner. They sat before the plantain leaves on which the food was served. To everyone's utter surprise, they ate the food from the leaves in a neat and clean manner, like men. They didn't bark or bite. They sat quietly until each one of them had finished, then got up and went

away as quietly as they had come.

The official was surprised and completely taken aback at the orderly behaviour of the dogs. Then Swamiji smiled and said, “Don’t think of them as ordinary dogs. They were high officials in their previous lives. But because of their corrupt practices, they are born as dogs in this life, to be ill-treated and looked upon with contempt by all. Who can escape the consequences of one’s actions?”

The official understood Swamiji’s subtle message. He was shamefaced and resolved from that day onwards not to be corrupt any more.

The Needle

When Guru Nanak was in Lahore, Duni Chand, a wealthy Hindu, invited him to eat with him. When Nanak approached Duni Chand's house, he saw seven metal flags fitted on the walls of the house. The Guru inquired about the purpose of the flags. He was told that each flag represented one lakh of rupees. That meant that Duni Chand was the master of rupees seven lakhs.

Guru Nanak wanted to steer Duni Chand away from the vanity of material riches. As soon as he entered the house, Duni Chand came forward to welcome him and show him the seat of honour.

Nanak then put a needle in his hand and said, "Keep it safe for me. I will take it from you when I want it."

Duni Chand was surprised at this strange request. Never the less, he took the needle with great devotion, thinking that it contained some miraculous powers. As he took the needle to keep it in a safe place, the Guru said, "Keep it very carefully. I will take it back from you in the next world."

In the next world! Duni Chand wondered what it implied. As he was keeping the needle in the safe, his wife came and asked him what he was doing. Duni Chand showed her the needle given by the Guru and said, "He will take it back from me in the next world."

The wife remonstrated, "Why did you agree to keep the needle for the Guru? How are you going to carry it to the next world? Have you ever seen anyone doing such an impossible thing? Please don't keep this needle with you. Return it to the Guru immediately."

Duni Chand understood his wife's logic. Immediately, he took the needle back to the Guru. He knelt before him and offering back the needle, said, "Please Sir, take back this needle. How can a needle be carried to the next world and returned to you? I will be committing a sin if I give you my word and fail to keep it."

Guru Nanak smiled and said, "Son, if this tiny needle cannot be carried into the next world, will you be able to carry with you your seven lakhs? Why are you wasting your life in accumulating this worthless wealth?"

From that day onwards, Duni Chand's passion for wealth decreased. He became a true devotee of the Lord and no longer took pride in the wealth and material comforts he had gathered around him.

Dharmavyadha

Once upon a time, there was a Brahmin boy who, returned home to his parents after finishing his education in his Guru's ashram. They were old and unable to run the household properly. So they said to him, "Son, marry a good girl now and settle down. If there is a daughter-in-law in the house, we will have some relief from the burden of work." But the son refused to get married. He wanted to be a recluse, live in the forest and gain yogic powers. So he left his old parents to their fate and went deep into a forest.

There he practised severe tapas. Sometimes he would go into a nearby village and beg for alms. Time passed. One day the brahmachari was sitting under a tree, practising austerities. The droppings of a crane, sitting on a branch of the same tree, fell on his head. He was disgusted and flashing with anger looked up at the crane. With that single look the bird was burnt and fell down dead!

The youth was greatly elated at this unexpected manifestation of his powers. "What tapobala!" He

congratulated himself for having attained such great siddhis. In a happy mood, he went into the village for bhiksha.

He stood before a merchant's house and cried out, *"bhavati bhiksham dehi,"* which meant, please give me some food.

The lady inside the house heard the cry and spoke from within, "Sir, please wait, I am busy. I shall come in a moment."

The brahmachari boiled in indignation. "What does she mean by keeping me waiting here? She doesn't know what a great person I am! Let her come out. I will show her," he thought.

After the lady completed her work, she was about to bring the bhiksha. Just then her husband returned home. As a wife dedicated to the service of her husband, she first attended to his needs. She fed him and made arrangements for his afternoon nap, and then brought the bhiksha. Meanwhile, the brahmachari waiting outside was becoming more and more angry. When the lady brought the food, he gave her a wrathful look.

The lady smiled sweetly at him and said, "Son, do you think I am a crane that I will get burnt by your look?" The brahmachari was dumbfounded! How did this lady know what had happened in the forest?

Forgetting all his anger, he asked humbly, "Mother, you appear to have great powers. How did you know what had happened in the forest? How did you gain this power?"

The lady said, "I know nothing about austere practices and yogas. I know only how to do my duty. Before marriage I served my parents with devotion. After marriage I have been serving my husband, considering him to be my God. I have no other claim to virtue. If you wish to know the why and the wherefore of it, go to the village yonder, where a certain butcher called Dharmavyadha lives. He will tell you everything."

Really! Could a butcher know anything about yoga? How could a man in such a hateful profession get such power? Curious, the brahmachari took leave of the lady, went to the next village and made enquiries about Dharmavyadha. He was guided to the meat-seller's shop. Unaccustomed to such sights he almost turned on his heels to retrace his steps. Just then, one of the shopkeepers looked at him and said, "Ah, you have been sent by the virtuous lady. Wait, Sir, I will come and talk to you shortly."

Here was a fresh surprise! How did the butcher know that the lady had sent him? He thought he had acquired great powers just by killing the crane with one look. Here were two ordinary persons doing no tapas at all, still they appeared to possess greater powers than him. He waited until the butcher closed his shop and came to him. Then they both went to his house together. The butcher seated the brahmachari in the hall and went to attend to his old dependent parents. After they were fed and comfortably put to bed, the butcher returned to the brahmachari.

By now the brahmachari had been properly humbled. He waited patiently until the butcher finished all his work and came to him. Then he asked, "How is it that even though you are so wise, you still follow the hateful profession of selling meat? Instead of going into the forest and acquiring more powers, why do you remain at home attending to a householder's duties?"

Dharmavyadha smiled and said, "Wisdom is gained by fulfilling and discharging one's duties in life and not by evading them. I am born in a family of butchers. There is nothing wrong in doing one's work in a detached manner."

Thus he taught the brahmachari the righteous way of living. Enlightened by the talk, he now understood how wrong he had been in neglecting his old parents. He was also remorseful because he had killed an innocent crane.

He took leave of Dharmavyadha and went straight back to his parents to become a householder and served them with love.

Wisdom and Action

Once, Narada brought a rare fruit and presented it to Lord Siva. The fruit was tempting to look at and had a wonderful fragrance. Siva's two sons, Vinayaka and Kumaraswamy, both ran to their father to claim it. There was only one fruit, Siva did not want to show any partiality by arbitrarily giving it to one of his sons. So he said that the fruit would go to the one who would be able to complete his journey around the earth first.

Kumaraswamy was very happy. He had a thin, athletic body and his vehicle was the swift peacock.

His elder brother Vinayaka had only a tiny mouse which struggled and groaned, while carrying his heavy body. He immediately jumped upon the peacock and flew off.

Poor Vinayaka was dejected. Why did his father have to arrange such an unequal race? By the time he looked for his mouse and started off, his brother would have already covered half the distance. Did his father love Kumara more than him? He sat and thought, butcould not think of a single occasion when his father had been partial to his brother. Then what did this mean? As he was brooding, it suddenly struck him that one need not physically run around the earth; there were other ways of doing it. He got up cheerfully, went around his parents three times and prostrated before them. Then he stood up and stretched out his hand for the fruit.

"Father, I have circled the earth thrice already. Give me the fruit," he said.

Lord Siva smiled at him and asked, "Explain how it is so."

Vinayaka replied, "Father, you and Mother are the Adidampati from whom the universe has emanated. All the worlds are in you. When I went around you once, it was equal to going around the earth once. I did so thrice. So I can say that I have circled the earth thrice."

Parameswara nodded His head in approval and gave the fruit to Vinakaya, who sat down comfortably in one corner, and slowly began to eat the fruit. He did not want to finish it before his brother came.

After some time Kumaraswamy returned triumphantly from his pradakshina, dreaming sweet dreams about the fruit. But, Vinayaka was already sitting there and finishing off the last bit of the fruit. In anger, Kumaraswamy went to his father and demanded an explanation. When he learnt that his elder brother had got the fruit by his fast thinking, instead of actually running around, he felt ashamed at his own lack of deep thinking. Vinayaka had truly won the contest by virtue of his superior intellect and Kumaraswamy had no choice but to accept defeat.

The Mirror

(Scene One)

(A villager called Rameshwar from a small village which has not yet been touched by modern civilisation, is walking in the streets of a big city, scared by all the new things he is seeing there. He is dressed in simple rustic clothes.)

Saroja Rameshwar

Rameshwar: *(Wonder-eyed)* O my God, how big is this city! How many new things! My head is reeling with all these. If I stay here for a fortnight, I will surely go mad. Poor Saroja! She has not seen such things. Had she been here she would have screamed with fright at all the mad things people do here. Ha, ha, ha! *(Suddenly he stops, seeing something on the road, shining and white)* What is this? It is bright and shining. *(Bends down and picks it up. It is a broken mirror. He has never seen a mirror before. In wonder* *he turns it round and round. He looks at its bright surface and sees his own face. Not knowing what it is, he immediately exclaims in joy)* Eh, father, you are here! Fifteen years ago when you died, they said that you had gone away to God and would not come back. How wonderful to meet you here!

I shall never leave you hereafter. Let me keep you safely. *(He takes the small towel thrown over his shoulder and carefully wrapping the mirror in it, ties it around his waist.)* Better not tell Saroja about my father. She will weep because her father is still lost. This time, I must be careful not to lose my father again. I will put him in my trunk and keep it locked. Otherwise he will go away again.

(As he walks along the road, he checks it now and then, touching his waist to make sure that his father is still there!)

(Curtain)

(Scene Two)

(In the village. Rameshwar enters his house and goes straight to the room where his clothes are kept. His wife Saroja follows as he opens the trunk.)

Saroja: Ah, you have come! How silently you came in. I didn't even notice. How did you like the big city? Was it very big? What did you see there?

Rameshwar: I will tell you presently. Now please go out. I have something to do.

Saroja: *(Surprised)* What is the urgency? If it is urgent, do it. Why should I go out?

Rameshwar: You must. I can't do it when you are here. *(He goes near her and catching hold of her hand, gently pushes her towards the door while she resists. But he is firm and strong. He sends her out of the door and then closes and bolts it. Then he carefully unties the garment around his waist and takes out the mirror. He looks into it to make sure that his father is still there)* Father, please don't leave me and go away this time. I was very young when you died. I never gave you due respect as I was very young then. But I promise not to neglect my duties hereafter. *(He opens his trunk and pulls out some clothes. From underneath he takes another small towel and wraps up the mirror carefully in it. He keeps the packet at the bottom and arranges his clothes over the packet. Then he closes the lid. He then gets up and opens the door. His wife, who has been waiting impatiently outside, comes in burning with curiosity.)*

Saroja: *(Suspiciously looking around)* What have you hidden here? Why did you close the door on me? What secrets do you keep from me?

Rameshwar: What secret? No secret at all. It is something that doesn't concern you. Don't worry about it. Do you know what all I saw in the city? Huge houses, one over the other. The one at the top is also as big as the house below. There are big and wonderful shops there. Come, I will show you what

I have brought for you. *(He leads her out. She looks back with suspicion as she is dragged out.)*

(Curtain)

(Scene Three)

(Early in the morning Rameshwar comes into his room and carefully closes and bolts the door. Then he opens the box and brings out the packet of towels containing the mirror and reverently keeps it on a stool and sits in front of it with closed eyes and joins his palms in prayer.)

Rameshwar: My dear father, bless me and my wife. May we come up in the world. May the cattle and the crops be good. May my children be strong and healthy. *(After the prayer he reverently prostrates in front of the mirror, wraps it up again and puts it back in the box and closes it. Then he gets up and opens the door. His wife comes in suspiciously and looks around.)*

Saroja: What are you doing here sitting all alone? I have been watching you for the last fifteen days. You lock yourself in the room every morning and come out after half an hour. What have you kept here secretly?

Rameshwar: You are imagining things. There is nothing here, secret or otherwise. Don't bother yourself with things that don't concern you.

Saroja: If there is nothing here, then why do you close the door? Have you ever done it before? You have started this ever since you returned from the city.

Rameshwar: It is all your imagination. There is nothing. What if I close the door? A man has several things to attend do. Why should women bother about them? *(He places his towel on his shoulder and goes out.)*

Saroja: *(Looks very worried)* There is surely something very wrong. Until now he has never hidden anything from me. Suddenly, why this secrecy? Today I must discover what it is.

(She carefully looks around, under and over every article in the room. Then she takes a key and opens the trunk. One by one, she takes out the clothes. Under the clothes she finds the packet and takes it out. She unwraps it and brings out the mirror. She doesn't know what it is and curiously turns it round and round. Then suddenly she sees her own face in it, but never having seen a mirror, is surprised to see a face in it and bursts into tears. She looks at the face again and again) So this is what he is doing. He has brought this woman from the city and hidden her here secretly. Every morning he locks the door and talks to her. *(Shedding angry tears)* Why did he need another woman? Am I not serving him properly? Don't I cook nice dishes for him? *(Just then her mother comes in)* Oh, Mother, how my husband wrongs me! He doesn't love me any more. He has got another woman in the house and every day he locks the door and talks to her. Mother, oh mother, I am lost! Who will look after me now? *(She starts lamenting loudly.)*

Mother: *(Holding her daughter with loving anxiety)* What did you say? Has he actually brought another woman into the house? Can he do so? Will the villagers allow it? Everyone will throw stones at him.

Saroja: *(Weeping bitterly, goes to the place where the mirror is and shows it to her mother)* See Mother, she is here.

Mother: *(She takes the mirror in her hand and turns it round and round and sees her own face in it. She is also seeing a mirror for the first time. After staring at it for some time)* What sort of a man is your husband? I can understand a man falling in love with younger and more beautiful girls. What did he see in this old hag? Her hair is white, her face is wrinkled and she is also toothless.

(In great sorrow, she embraces her daughter and weeps along with her) My girl, I have spoiled your whole life by giving you in marriage to this man. The shameless creature! He has gone to the city just once and he brings an old woman as a rival to you. How unfortunate you are, my daughter. Why do you need to face such troubles while you are still so young!

Rameshwar: *(Returns from outside and finds the mother and daughter weeping. He comes near anxiously)* What is the matter? Why are you both weeping? Is there any bad news from anywhere?

Saroja: *(In anger)* Look at him! As if he doesn't know! Having done such a shameless thing he questions us. Why did you bring her? Am I not faithful to you? Am I not good looking enough for you? Have I ever given you any trouble? Is this the way you repay my devotion to you?

Mother: How long do you expect us to bear it? You have my beautiful daughter and you need an old hag too? Do you think you will get away with such behaviour?

Rameshwar: *(Completely bewildered)* What are you blabbering about? Have you both gone mad? What is this talk about bringing a girl home? I have not brought anyone at all.

Saroja: No? *(Showing the mirror defiantly)* Then who is this? How dare you deny it? Did you think that we were so ignorant that we would not discover your secret affair? We know all about it!

Rameshwar: *(Grabbing the mirror)* Why did you take him out? That is my father there, not a woman. I worship him every day.

Saroja: Your father? Why do you try to bluff? Does your father wear ear rings and a necklace? Does he put a tilak on his forehead?

Mother: Does he have long white hair?

Saroja: Does he wear a sari?

Mother: Son-in-law, we know better than to be hoodwinked by you. I am not going to take this lying down. We will inform all the elders of the village and make them reprimand you. We may look helpless but we are not!

Rameshwar: *(Enraged)* You silly fools! You don't know what you are blabbering. In the city I found my father and brought him home. Though he does not talk to me, he looks at me and smiles.

Saroja: I know, I know you talk to her and worship her every day, the she-devil! *(Weeping, she embraces her mother)* Mother, he doesn't need me any more. Take me away from here. I shall jump into a well and commit suicide.

Mother: *(In bitterness)* No. Why should you die for his misbehaviour? Come, we will go to Guru Maharaj. He will know how to punish him. Eh, son-in-law, come. We won't leave you. *(Between them, the mother and the daughter push and pull him. They then exit along with the mirror.)*

(Curtain)

(Scene Four)

(In the Guru's ashram, a white-haired Swami is seen sitting on the takht. In front of him seven or eight men and women are sitting. Swamiji is talking and others are listening.)

Guruji: The world and a man's life are both sacred gifts of God. We should know how to worship God through both. But lost in delusion, we torture and tease one another and waste our precious lives.

(Mother and Saroja, dragging a reluctant Rameshwar, enter. He, loudly protesting, and they shouting. Swamiji's talk is disturbed and they all look at the approaching group.)

Rameshwar: Why have you dragged me here? I told you I worship my father. You imagine things and accuse me. Leave me alone!

Saroja: Yes, yes, we will leave you when you leave the she-devil.

Mother: You wish to be free to do injustice to my innocent daughter! What else? *(By this time they all come near Guruji and prostrate.)*

Maharaj, look at this son-in-law of mine! I gave my daughter to him four years ago. She is very obedient to him and serves him with love. Fifteen days ago he went to the city and brought back another woman with him.

Rameshwar: I told you that I brought back my father, not a woman.

Saroja: *(Weeping loudly)* Father, Father! His father was dead and gone fifteen years ago. Guruji, how can he bring back his father? He brought with him a young woman, and sits with her every day behind locked doors. *(Sobbing inconsolably)* Mother, I have no desire to live any more. I will burn myself and die. Let him be happy with his sweetheart.

Rameshwar: *(Looking at the Guru bewildered)*

Guru Maharaj, it is my father I worship daily. I found him after fifteen years when I was walking on the streets. I found him in the city and brought him home. Mother and daughter are making false accusations against me.

Guruji: *(Looks at all three of them keenly and asks)* You say that your husband brought a woman and kept her in the house? *(Saroja nods)* Where is she?

Saroja: *(Hands over the mirror)* Here, Maharaj. The she-fox is here!

Mother: She is not even a nice young girl, Guruji, but an ugly old hag. I don't know what my son-in-law saw in her.

Rameshwar: It is my father, Guru Maharaj. These women talk nonsense.

(Guruji takes the mirror in his hand and looks into it. He sees his own face. He understands the whole mistake and what the quarrel is all about. He laughs uproariously. They all look at him surprised.)

Guruji: *(Still laughing and looking at them kindly)* My dears, there is nothing to worry about. Don't be sad, Daughter. Don't be worried, Mother. Your daughter is not in any danger. Your son-in-law hasn't done anything wrong. *(All of them look happy)* Now look, you are quarrelling about this, isn't it? *(Shows them the mirror. They all nod their head)* Is it possible for a man to be so small? *(Rameshwar shakes his* *head)* Is it possible for a woman to be so small? *(Saroja and her mother shake their head.)*

Guruji: So let me tell you what this is. It is called a mirror. It shows only your own face!

All three: *(In disbelief)* My face?

Guruji: *(Smiling)* Yes, your own face. Now all of you sit in a straight line, facing me. *(They sit in a straight line, side by side, facing the Guru.)*

Guruji: Good. Now look. *(He holds the mirror in front of them. All of them look and are wonderstruck.)*

The three: There, my father, Look, the she-devil, There, the old hag.

Guruji: *(Laughs)* Son, you salute your father.

Rameshwar: *(Joins the palms and salutes Gurudev)* My father is also saluting!

Guruji: Daughter, you smile!

Saroja: *(Smiles)* Guruji, She is also smiling!

Guruji: Mother, you touch your head with your hand.

Mother: *(Touches her head with her hand)* Why, Guruji, the old woman is also doing the same.

Guruji: So, now you understand, don't you? There is no one here. It is only your own face that you see reflected in the mirror. Watch carefully. Daughter, don't you see your husband? Rameshwar, is this not your wife? And is not the other one your mother-in-law?

The three: *(Together)* Yes, Guruji, indeed they are our own faces! *(They all laugh uproariously. Guruji smiles.)*

Rameshwar: *(Laughing)* I worshipped myself thinking it was my father!

Saroja: *(Laughing)* Oh, I considered myself as my own rival and became jealous!

Mother: *(Laughing with shame)* I condemned myself as an old hag! *(Laughing, they take leave of Guruji and go away.)*

Guruji: *(Smiling, turns to the devotees)* You have witnessed how misunderstandings grow. The world is nothing but a reflection of our own minds. If you see it as bad, it is because your mind is bad. If you see it as good, it is because your own mind is good. Make the mind perfect, you will see a perfect world before you!

(Curtain)

Savitri

(Scene One)

Savitri

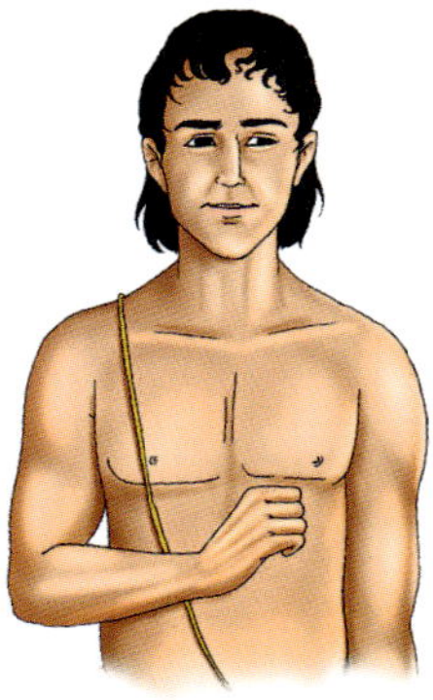

Satyavana

Yama

(In the palace of Ashwapati. King Ashwapati is seated in the hall. His queen and minister are with him. They appear to be in a serious conversation.)

Queen: My Lord, our daughter Savitri is of marriageable age. If it pleases you, it is time to find a husband for her.

Ashwa: You are right. It is a wonder that so far no one has come forward to claim her hand. Does a jewel seek buyers? The buyers should be anxious to get the jewel.

Minister: The princes would have vied with one another, O King, had the princess been merely beautiful and nothing more. But her splendour and qualities are so extraordinary that all normal princes do not consider themselves good enough for her.

Ashwa: *(Looking worried)* So my girl remains unwed! Let us give her the choice to choose her own life partner. *(Claps his hands. A servant appears)* Convey to the princess that we desire to see her. *(The servant bows and withdraws returning with Savitri.)*

Savitri: *(Comes and bows to her parents)* Did you send for me, Father?

Ashwa: Savitri, let me be frank with you. We are worried about not finding a suitable bridegroom for you. Your beauty and grace are so overwhelming that all the princes fear to seek your hand. Take your maids and a thousand strong army and go from kingdom to kingdom to make the choice of your heart. I promise to abide by your decision and wed you to the man of your choice.

Savitri: Anything you wish, Father. *(She bows and leaves.)*

(Curtain)

(Scene Two)

(Savitri enters and prostrates before her parents. They embrace her and bid her to sit.)

Ashwa: We are glad that you have returned from your quest. Have you found someone suitable enough to be your husband?

Savitri: *(Smiling with bent head)* I went from kingdom to kingdom, father, but everywhere I met with disappointment. Shallowness of outlook alone met my eyes wherever I went. I was disillusioned and was returning home when ... *(Falters with shyness.)*

Queen: *(Patting her daughter on the back with her hand)* When ... ? Speak, Savitri. We are eager to hear all about it.

Savitri: *(With a shy smile)* While returning I saw a youthful prince gathering fruit in the forest. On enquiry we found, Mother ... *(Again stops out of shyness.)*

Ashwa: *(Eagerly)* Yes my daughter, who is the prince? What is his name and which kingdom does he belong to?

Savitri: His father is no more a king. He lost his kingdom and is now in the forest in exile. He is King Dyumatsena, and Satyavana is the prince's name. The prince serves his parents who are both old and blind.

Queen: Is the prince handsome and virtuous, Savitri?

Savitri: I found him so, Mother. Serene and calm, unruffled by ups and downs in life, he is cheerful and also dutiful to his parents. I feel that life with such a man would be worthwhile.

Narada: *(Enters singing. All of them get up and prostrate before the sage and take their seats only after Narada is seated)* O King, you appear to be in the middle of a serious conference.

Ashwa: Divine sage, what is there to hide from you? My daughter Savitri has just returned from a journey and has chosen a young prince as her husband. She was just telling us about it. Your arrival is indeed a godsend for us. Please tell us whether prince Satyavana, the son of Dyumatsena is suitable for her.

Narada: *(Closes his eyes and thinks for a moment)* King Satyavana is good, handsome and fit for Savitri in every respect. But ... alas ... *(Stops.)*

Ashwa: *(Anxiously)* Yes, Devarshi, what is it? Is there any hitch? *(The queen and Savitri look at Narada eagerly.)*

Narada: I do not wish to say it, Ashwapati, but the boy is destined to die exactly one year from this day.

All: *(Exclaim in sorrow)* What?

Narada: His life-span is short. Destiny is inexorable, O King.

Ashwa: *(With regret, turning to Savitri)* My child, you have heard what Devarshi said. Please choose another prince.

Savitri: *(Aghast)* O no, Father! Once her heart is given can a woman marry another? I already consider him my husband.

Queen: *(With tears)* Savitri, how can we see you rendered a widow! Your whole life will be a river of sorrow, my child.

Ashwa: My daughter, we were childless for long. We worshipped the effulgent Goddess Savitri and you were given to us as Her boon. You are the light of our eyes. Our lives will be useless if any inauspiciousness befalls you. Give up this ill-fated marriage and choose another husband.

Savitri: *(Tearful, but shaking her head)* Dear Father, do not grieve for me. Born out of the boon of the effulgent one, how can I have tragedy in life? Please trust in the Divine Mother, and wed me to the prince. I can never think of another man. Please do not force me, Father!

Ashwa: *(Turns to Devarshi in misery)* Devarshi, give us good counsel. I am not able to think coherently.

Narada: O King, do not be anxious, but carry out Savitri's wish. True, Satyavana is destined to die, but nothing can be impossible for a pativrata. Who knows, perhaps, Savitri can get back her husband from the jaws of death. *(All the three bow down before Narada who blesses them.)*

(Curtain)

(Scene Three)

(In the forest Dyumatsena's parnashala. The blind parents are seen seated on a cot. Satyavana is preparing to go to the forest for fuel. Savitri brings milk to the parents-in-law and stands nearby as they drink. After they finish she takes the tumblers from their hands and kneels before them.)

Savitri: Father, may I go to the forest today, along with my husband? I have never been there before. I desire to see the wondrous beauties of the forest.

Dyumat: Daughter, you have been fasting for the last three days and are much emaciated. Take rest today. Some other day you may certainly go.

Mother: Savitri, in this one year you have never asked us for anything. I do not wish to deny this first desire expressed by you. But as your father said, you are very weak with the constant work that you have to do and the fasting of the last three days. Wait for a few days more, then you will be strong enough.

Savitri: Mother, please do not deny my request. Today, of all days, I wish to accompany him to the forest. Father, I am not feeling weak at all. Even if

I feel giddy, your son will be there to look after me. Please permit me to go.

Dyumat: Well Daughter, if you desire, do go. *(Calling Satyavana)* Son, Savitri wishes to accompany you today. Don't go very far. She is weak after her fast. She won't be able to walk far.

Satya: Yes, Father. We will not go too far. Come, Savitri. *(They both bow to the parents.)*

(Curtain)

(Scene Four)

(Savitri and Satyavana enter the forest. Savitri has a flower basket and Satyavana is carrying an axe.)

Satyavana: *(Getting a flower)* See, this is the Kinshuka flower. How red it is, like the blush on the cheeks of a bride.

Savitri: *(Taking the flower in hand and examining it closely)* How wonderful is Mother Nature! Untouched by man, the forest presents the most breathtaking scenes. Look at those white birds flying in the sky. Aryaputra! They are dividing the blue sky into two halves.

Satyavana: *(Looking up)* Yes, what a lovely sight! Savitri, we have walked long enough. You won't be able to take any more strain. Let us stop here. I shall chop the wood. Meanwhile you can amuse yourself by gathering flowers.

Savitri: Yes, Aryaputra. That is a good idea.

(Satyavana starts chopping wood, while Savitri moves around collecting flowers. She goes out by one exit and comes back, carefully watching Satyavana all the while. After some time, Satyavana drops the axe from his hand and wipes his brow. He looks weak and dazed.)

Satyavana: *(Clutching his head with both his hands)* Savitri, my dear. Where are you? Something is the matter with me.

Savitri: *(Comes running. She drops the basket and rushes to hold Satyavana)* Aryaputra, what has happened? Are you hurt?

Satyavana: No, suddenly some strange weakness has come over me, I am hardly able to stand. My head is reeling and I am in a daze. Help me, I am falling. *(He slumps slowly while Savitri helps him to lie on the ground with his head on her lap.)*

Savitri: How do you feel now? *(Satyavana lies still and gives no reply. Savitri anxiously feels his pulse which is beating slower and feebler. Suddenly at the feet of Satyavana a black effulgent figure is visible with a noose in hand. Savitri sees him and shudders.)*

Savitri: *(Joining her palms in salutation)* O resplendent one, shining like the sun, who are you? Whence have you come?

Yama: *(Surprised)* You are able to see me? It must be because of your purity. Savitri, know me to be Yamadharmaraja, who has come to take away Satyavana's life. Today he has to die. As he is an extremely truthful and pious man, I have come personally to take him. *(He throws his noose over the body of Satyavana and turns to go.)*

(Curtain falls and rises. Another part of the forest is seen. Yama walking in front and Savitri is following him.)

Yama: *(Turns back and sees Savitri)* Savitri, why are you following me? Go back. This is no place for young girls like you.

Savitri: Yamaraj, is there a dharma unknown to you? Is not the right place of a woman by the side of her husband? You are carrying away my husband. How can I remain behind?

Yama: O righteous one, the living wife follows the husband till he is alive. She cannot cross the realm of life and follow him into death. Go back. It is futile to seek him.

Savitri: The scriptures say that the wife follows her husband through seven lives. I am but obeying the scriptures when I follow my husband.

Yama: I am pleased with your righteous conduct, O Savitri. Ask for a boon other than your husband's life. It shall be granted.

Savitri: My parents-in-law are blind and in exile having lost their kingdom. O Yamadharmaraja, grant that they may get back both their vision and the lost kingdom.

Yama: So be it! Now turn back, Savitri. You have come very far. *(Yama turns and goes forward. Savitri follows.)*

(Curtain falls and rises again showing them in another part of a forest.)

Yama: *(Turns back and sees Savitri)* Savitri, why are you still following me? These lands are not meant for the wanderings of delicate girls. Return to the realm of human beings.

Savitri: After seven steps have been taken together, seven words have been spoken together, only then friendships are made. I had the good fortune to walk with you for more than seven steps and speak more than seven words. So you are now my friend.

Yama: *(Smiling)* Savitri, I am happy with your knowledge of the sastras and your adherence to it.

Ask a boon other than your husband's life. It shall be yours.

Savitri: My father has no children apart from me. O controller and ruler of men! Grant that my father may have a hundred sons.

Yama: So be it. Now turn back, Savitri. You have come far beyond the regions of human existence. Go back.

(Yama goes his way. Savitri follows him. Curtain comes down and rises again, showing Yama and Savitri in the vicinity of Yama-loka, which is seen in the background.)

Yama: *(Turning back and seeing Savitri still following)* Savitri, you are still with me! These are the grounds where no human being has ever trod. This is the world of the dead which no living being can cross. Return to your world, my child.

Savitri: You are known as Yama, because you are the controller of all. You are called Samavarti because you are equal to all. You are pointed out as Dharmaraja because you are the righteous upholder of dharma. What fear is there for me where you, the effulgent one, exists? I am following dharma; I am following my husband. Where these two are present, it is no alien land for me.

Yama: *(Looking happy)* Savitri, you are indeed the embodiment of wisdom and dharma. Ask any boon other than your husband's life.

Savitri: O mighty controller! Grant that I may have a hundred sons.

Yama: So be it! Now go back. No one can pass these barriers and go beyond. *(Turns back and goes forward. Savitri follows. After a few paces, Yama sees her still following)* My daughter, why are you still following me?

Savitri: You are the most truthful and righteous of all. Hence it is that you are in charge of the lives of men. O Yamadharmaraja, you have given me the boon of sons. How can I have sons without my husband?

Yama: *(Taken aback for a minute, laughs good-humouredly)* Ah, Savitri, you have won. Here, I give back the life of your husband. *(He opens his noose and lets out the subtle body of Satyavana)* Go back and live happily with your husband.

(Savitri gratefully prostrates before Yamadharmaraja and goes back. Curtain drops down and rises again showing the place where Satyavana is lying. Savitri enters quickly. She sits down near Satyavana and gently lifts his head and places it in her lap and awaits for him to wake up.)

Satyavana: *(Slowly breathes, then moves and finally opening his eyes smiles at Savitri and sits up)* Oh my dear, what a strange dream I had. I dreamt that I was dead and was being taken away by Yamadharmaraja; that you followed me and got my life back from him. It is so vivid that I can't brush it off as a dream. Tell me, is it true? Did you fight for my life and get me back?

Savitri: *(Happily looking at him)* Aryaputra, it is my good fortune that you have come back to me alive and well. It is already late. Your parents will be waiting anxiously for us. Let us make haste.

(They get up and collect the wood, axe and flower basket and start walking.)

(Curtain)

CODE OF CONDUCT FOR THE CHINMAYA MISSION MEMBERS

By thought, word and deed, every member of the Chinmaya Mission, should try to live up to and fulfill the motto as well as the pledge of the Mission.

- He should spare time daily to do meditation and study the scriptures.
- Once a week, on any convenient day, he must offer worship at a nearby temple with the members of his family.
- He should first discover a life of harmony at home. It is expected of him that he does not, on any account, create any domestic unhappiness.
- If there are children at home, he will have, at least once a week, a satsang at home, consisting mainly of members of the family, wherein reading of itihasas like Ramayana and Mahabharata or Puranas like Bhagavata in a language the children know, would form an important part.
- When he meets another Mission member, he greets him with Hari Om.
- Daily offering of pranams to the elders in the house by the younger ones should be followed and inculcated by the Mission members.

CHINMAYA MISSION PLEDGE

We stand as one family
bound to each other with love and respect.

We serve as an army,
courageous and disciplined,
ever ready to fight against
all low tendencies and false values,
within and without us.

We live honestly
the noble life of sacrifice and service,
producing more than what we consume,
and giving more than what we take.

We seek the Lord's grace
to keep us on the path of virtue, courage and
wisdom.

May Thy grace and blessings
flow through us to the world around us.

We believe that the service of our country is the
service of the Lord of Lords
and devotion to the people
is the devotion to the supreme Self.

We know our responsibilities;
Give us the ability and courage
to fulfill them.

Om Tat Sat